BEEKEEPING FOR BEGINNERS

A Beginner's Guide on How to Understand the Basics and Get Started With Beekeeping

Text Copyright © Light Bulb Publishing

All rights reserved. No part of this guide may be reproduced in any form without permission in writing from the publisher except in the case of brief quotations embodied in critical articles or reviews.

Legal & Disclaimer

The information contained in this book and its contents is not designed to replace or take the place of any form of medical or professional advice; and is not meant to replace the need for independent medical, financial, legal or other professional advice or services, as may be required. The content and information in this book has been provided for educational and entertainment purposes only.

The content and information contained in this book has been compiled from sources deemed reliable, and it is accurate to the best of the Author's knowledge, information, and belief. However, the Author cannot guarantee its accuracy and validity and cannot be held liable for any errors and/or omissions. Further, changes are periodically made to this book as and when needed. Where appropriate and/or necessary, you must consult a professional (including but not limited to your doctor, attorney, financial advisor or such other professional advisor) before using any of the suggested remedies, techniques, or information in this book.

Upon using the contents and information contained in this book, you agree to hold harmless the Author from and against any damages, costs, and expenses, including any legal fees potentially resulting from the application of any of the information provided by this book. This disclaimer applies to any loss, damages or injury caused by the use and application, whether directly or indirectly, of any advice or information presented, whether for breach of contract, tort, negligence, personal injury, criminal intent, or under any other cause of action.

You agree to accept all risks of using the information presented in this book.

You agree that by continuing to read this book, where appropriate and/or necessary, you shall consult a professional (including but not limited to your doctor, attorney, or financial advisor or such other advisor as needed) before using any of the suggested remedies, techniques, or information in this book.

Table of Contents

Introduction 1
   About this Manual 1
   What is Beekeeping? 2
   What is its impact on the world? 3
   Who are your co-beekeepers? 4

What You Need to Start 5
   Bee Source 5
   Proper Location 9
   Beekeeping Equipment 11
      The Hive and Its Components 11
      Protective Suit 19
      Smoker 21
      Hive Tools 23
   Rules/Regulations 25

The Bee & Bee Caste 27
   Bee Anatomy 27
   Pheromones 30
   Bee Caste 31
      Queen 33
      Drones 36
      Workers 37
      The Brood 42

Establishment & Management 45
   Establishment 45
   Management (Seasonal) 46

Spring and Summer 47
Post-Winter/Pre-Spring 47
    Feeding 47
    Inspection 50
    Cnidophobia 52
    Supering 52
    Supersedure 53
    Swarming 55
    Splitting 57
Autumn and Winter 59
    Autumn Feeding 60
    Robbing 61
Pests and Diseases 62
    Mites 62
    American Foulbrood 64
    European Foulbrood 65
    Nosema 66

Honey and Beeswax 67
Honey Properties 67
    Harvest and Storage 68
Beeswax 70
    Rendering 70

Beekeeping Benefits 71
Health 71
Economic Returns 71

Conclusion 73

Introduction

About this Manual

Beekeeping is a necessary practice to keep food production sustainable. The purpose of this manual is to teach beginners how to practically apply beekeeping principles to their practices.

Like other Beekeeping for Beginners books circulating on the internet and in libraries, we will teach you general lessons on how to start beekeeping. Referencing others' practices and principles, we have collated all the most valuable techniques in modern beekeeping.

This book is the result of years of family experience and professional practice. We are bringing you the most up-to-date guide to start your own bee-venture. Be it a future business goal or a hobby, this book will help you begin beekeeping.

What is Beekeeping?

Beekeeping is a practice carried out by farmers, scientists, hobbyists, and businesspersons around the world for various personal and commercial purposes. It is the process of domesticating bees in order to collect their products or assist with pollinating crops in the field. We keep bees for products like beeswax, jelly, pollen and propolis (bee glue). However, honey is the most popular product created by bees.

Beekeeping is a process intended to mimic the lives of bees in nature. Instead of letting them build natural combs in places near human properties, we keep bee colonies in manufactured hives. **Hives** are wooden structures that bees decide to live in. A **colony** is a family of bees consisting of castes. Bees hosted in these hives are usually *Apis millefera* or simply, honeybees.

Apiculturists/apiarists keep bees for large-scale purposes, following strict processes for replenishment of the bee population for the purposes of pollination and honey production. Some beekeepers sell their bees and beekeeping equipment to other beekeepers to help them start their own practices.

Humans have been eating honey for a long time. We started to keep bees in pottery vessels in North Africa 9,000 years ago, which led to modern day beekeeping.

Photo courtesy: Damien Tupinier

What is its impact on the world?

The global bee population has drastically declined and continues to do so. Albert Einstein believed that humanity would have four years to live after the disappearance of bees. Without bees, we would not have enough plants to convert energy into the food that every living organism needs to survive.

If you care about nature, then beekeeping is an easy and beneficial hobby for you to take up. A hive or two is the best way to start. When we started our own beekeeping venture, we had five hives, and now we have an apiary. These days, our countryside farmers mostly have a few hives to maintain pollination (and for honey, of course).

This process is an integral part of the agriculture and food production industries. An average hive of 30,000 bees can visit 150 million flowers per day. Though not all of these flowers will produce fruits for human consumption, they will help secure our farms' produce and serve as a nutrient source for other animals and insects.

Beekeeping is necessary in sustainable agriculture and permaculture. The death of bees would have a devastating effect on agriculture. By helping the most efficient pollinators survive, we are helping plants proliferate and produce food for every living entity on the planet.

Who are your co-beekeepers?

Every state has its own community of beekeepers. The American Beekeeping Federation and United States Department of Agriculture will always be there to guide you. Beekeepers today have some different ideas about beekeeping; they don't all agree on everything. Every area is unique and the bees' performance can vary depending on local climate and flora. Understanding your bees requires profound skill, which you can gain through experience and time.

According to US law, there should be two bee inspectors per state, but not all states can comply with this due to lack of availability. We highly suggest you network with the beekeepers in your region by visiting their apiary sites prior to starting your practice.

There are thousands of beekeepers you can learn from and countless resources online. Experience will always be the best teacher and that comes from those who have been doing it for years. Cooperation with other beekeepers will help you succeed.

What You Need to Start

Bee Source

You can acquire your bees in many ways. The three best bee sources are: established hives, package bees, and nuc colonies.

a. **Established hives** (second hives) are best because everything is already set up by an experienced beekeeper. You are technically buying a hive he or she has been strengthening for years. If you get it early in spring or late winter, and if the colony is doing an excellent job of reproducing, you can add another hive around summer, which will help you get to know your bees better. This is an excellent choice which allows you to study the hive and apply the practices and concepts you will learn from this guide.

Photo courtesy: Ali Can

It already has stored honey and the pollen the bees and brood (eggs and small bees) need to settle in. However, this is the most expensive option of the three. It runs from $350 to $400 not including other materials.

b. **Package bees,** as seen on the left, are a cheaper option. It is a huge box with a caged queen, bee workers and an artificial feed made out of sugar. This is the only way you can order them online because of the secure packaging.

Usually, two pounds of bees run from $95 to $135, and three pounds cost $130 to $160. You can easily dump them into your hive.

We do not recommend this bee source to new beekeepers since the colony will have to adapt to its new environment and create its comb from scratch. If not properly set up, worker bees may reject the queen bee due to the stress from shipment and change of environment. The quality of sperm deposited in the queen also degrades severely during shipment.

It is imperative that the hive accepts the queen because it cannot survive without her.

Some beekeepers cover the queen in a food plug. The workers will meet their queen by eating the food plug, working their way in if they accept her as their queen. Package bees are recommended for when you are losing worker bees in an already set-up and maintained hive. However, there are cases in which introduced workers are rejected by the hive. Package bees can help you grow your apiary site after years of experience.

What You Need to Start

c. The third and most common way of sourcing your bees is through **nucleus hives** (nuc hives). A nuc hive is a smaller, temporary functioning beehive. It is a bit more expensive than the last option, running from $150 to $300 per nuc colony depending on the state it comes from. Bees from nuc hives are all close relatives with offspring hatching from the laying queen.

Sadly, diseases and insects that are present from the seller will likely tag along as well. This is the biggest disadvantage. However, there is no possibility of queen rejection.

This is why you need to be on the lookout before ordering any kind of colony. Not many shipping agencies ship colonies. However, this is actually helpful because you get to see the status of the hives yourself when you visit a bee supplier. You can find them through friends or your local government office.

It is best to pre-order bees before January or February, as stocks are limited and it allows the beekeepers to strengthen your future colony in preparation for its adaptation to the new environment.

This book assumes that Western/European honeybees (*Apis mellifera*) are what you plan to domesticate. This is a no-brainer because even if you want to keep other bee species, only *Apis mellifera* can produce honey. This might be confusing, but the Italian honeybee is in fact a subspecies of the Western/European honeybee; its complete scientific name is *Apis mellifera ligustica*. They are mostly the same but the Italian bee is preferred by most beekeepers today. Other subspecies commonly kept in the US are Carniolan, Caucasian, and Russian honeybees.

Proper Location

Later in this chapter, we will discuss rules and regulations for starting your beekeeping venture. In the meantime, let's discuss where to set your apiary or honey beehives up.

The location of your honeybee sites is important. Before introducing new colonies, evaluate these factors first: foraging opportunities, sources of nectar and pollen, water, sunshine, wind, and safety from pesticides, animals, natural calamities, and diseases. You might also want to keep vehicle accessibility and the possibility of angry neighbors in mind.

Most beekeeper hobbyists live in residential and suburban areas. If you are living in one, make sure not to bother your neighbors when you work with bees. Please inform them of what you are doing, in case they have allergies.

When you introduce honeybees into your new site, worker bees will immediately scout the area for nectar and pollen. There should be a food source within five to ten miles. This is one of the benefits of buying nuc or established colonies – the bees already have a source of food in the hive in case they must fly a long distance in the new area.

If there is no natural body of water nearby, set up a pan of water with stones for the bees to land on. Water also helps regulate hive temperature during the hot summer months and is critical for raising the brood.

An open field for sunshine is essential, so light can creep inside and the nurse bees can see eggs easily. Shade affects the flight of bees and helps regulate the surrounding humidity. There must be protection from the wind by natural barriers such as hills, evergreens, trees or buildings.

Pesticides negatively affect the physiological functions of bees. If you decide to do beekeeping as a business and register as organic, make sure the farms nearby follow natural farming practices, because the approval of your business permit (organic enterprise) will depend on the pollen the bees collect. Pesticides from nearby farms are a big no-no.

Animals such as pets, bears, reptiles and rodents are always a menace. Especially in the far North, bears can smell and ransack your hive when you least expect it.

By elevating hives above the ground using cement blocks or wood stands, you can protect against rodents and weather conditions such as floods and hurricanes. Strong winds can topple hives if they're on poorly constructed bases.

Beekeeping Equipment

This is one of the most important parts of this manual. We highly recommend that you conduct further study on the features and usage of all the equipment you will need for beekeeping. The main equipment includes the hive and its components, protective suit, smoker and hive tools.

The Hive and Its Components

The hive does not only house your bee colony but also the overall success of your project. Maintenance of its components will ensure long-term success and profitable gains. Protection of the hive from insects, termites and wood diseases means protecting your investment as well.

The hive's five basic components are stand, body, super, frames and outer cover.

There are four different types of beehives: the Langstroth, Warre, Long Horizontal Hive and Top Bar. Your beekeeping management style will depend on which type of beehive you decide to use. For the sake of this beginner's guide, we will talk about the one that is most widely used today - the Langstroth. Most modern beekeepers use this for its practical efficiency and dynamic features.

The **hive stand** is a thick base of wood on top your constructed elevation. Wood diseases may come from floodwater slipping in crevices and weakening the foundation. The stand should be sturdy so that when you add more bodies or compartments on top, it is strong enough to support the whole structure.

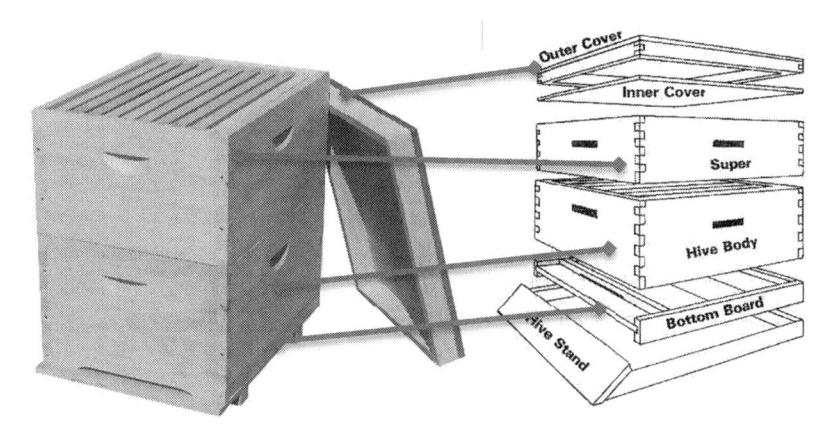

Wooden-hive box (Beeplaza)

The **bottom board** serves as the floor of the hive. It has a rectangular wooden extension that serves as a landing and takeoff platform for working foragers. It should have a customizable wide opening with an entrance reducer you can add and remove at any time. An entrance reducer is a piece of block that covers the entrance, leaving an inch or two of space for bees to go in and out. Woodworkers purposely tilt the bottom board to keep rainwater from flowing in. In most of my hives, we add divisions in the opening to keep mice out. Some beehives have a steel–plate division that clicks to the top when you want to leave the entrance open, and clicks back down when closed.

Today, bottom boards are customized with a screen inside as an Integrated Pest Management (IPM) practice to collect mites that have fallen off bees when they clean themselves. We apply oil on the IPM platform so the mites get stuck and you can pull them out to eradicate the pest. It can also give you information about the inside the hive, such as dripping honey from the hanging frames, or wax scraps eaten by emerging young bees.

Hive-makers mostly use pinewood but we highly recommend cypress wood because of its decay-resistant property. We painted ours to protect it from the heat and rain. For inventory and management purposes, you can color your hives.

The **hive body** is a four-sided outer compartment of the hive with internal extended bars where we hang frames on both sides. What we call the hive body depends on its use and size. There are three sizes: deep, medium and shallow.

Deep bodies are the biggest and are always on top of the bottom board. We call it the brood box when we use it for brood rearing. The queen lives here, spending most of her day laying eggs. This is where all the bees begin as eggs and become fully functioning adults for the hive, such as drones (male bees) or workers (female bees).

The next compartment is the **super,** which can also be deep, medium or shallow depending on how we need it. Supers are where bees produce surplus honey for consumption. The queen doesn't lay eggs in the super because beekeepers include another part called the queen excluder. This is to limit her to laying eggs in the main body and not wandering around the upper chambers instead. Thus, bees only use these super frames (medium or shallow) for storing honey as an extra food source.

Some beekeepers do not suggest having a queen excluder, as some believe beekeeping is not just a business but also a cause to help increase the bee population.

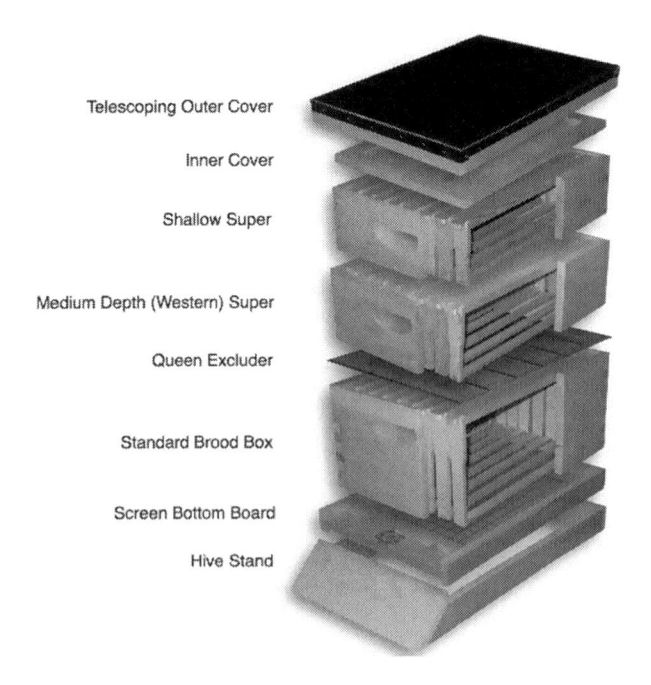

Telescoping Outer Cover
Inner Cover
Shallow Super
Medium Depth (Western) Super
Queen Excluder
Standard Brood Box
Screen Bottom Board
Hive Stand

Photo courtesy: Oregon State Beekeepers Association

Single hive management means you can have one standard brood box, whereas double brood box management means you can add two deep bodies for the queen to lay more eggs. With double brood, we add two or three shallow supers for more honey. If the bees are healthy and there is space to fill, they will draw more combs and fill them with honey.

Frames are the rectangular wooden objects within which bees build their combs. Each body contains ten frames. However, some beekeepers prefer the eight-frame body (not as heavy) to provide more ventilation and less contact on hot summer days. Going back to our bee source, nuc hives only have four to five frames, established hives may differ depending on your agreement with the beekeeper, and package bees have no frames.

We build frames following a specific measurement (Langstroth's contribution to the world of Beekeeping). The sizes for each type follow the sizes of the body, which are also deep, medium and shallow.

The horizontal length of all top and lower bars is 19 inches long by 1 1/16 inches on one side and 3/4 inches of bar thickness on the other side.

The vertical length (height) of the frame shows the exact size whether your frame is deep, medium or shallow:

a. Shallows are 5 3/8 inches

b. Mediums are 6 1/4 inches

c. Deeps are 9 1/8 inches

We also have something we call bee space (exactly 3/8 inch) between each frame. Its purpose is to keep bees from building combs in between.

The **inner cover** is found above the topmost super just beneath the outer cover. The inner cover may be replaced by other components depending on its use to aid the activities of the hive when the weather changes.

The inner cover may be made of flexible cloth, steel or wood. In a natural environment, bees start to create combs by secreting beeswax on the ceiling surface or sides and work the comb downward. We do not want them doing that in the hive. To prevent this, we place an inner cover before the outer one.

The **outer cover** protects the entire hive from rain leaks and other external factors. It must be sturdy and customizable with a moisture board to help control moisture inside the hive.

Let us return to the frames.

Frames come in three different types: empty, wired, and plastic or wax foundation. The ones you buy from commercial stores are the wooden empty frames. However, you don't need to worry about this because hive bodies usually come with frames.

In empty frames, bees can freely build their combs in the middle, resulting in wavy, lumpy and uneven clusters of cells, which are difficult to remove for hive inspection. When the uneven protruding parts hit the other drawn comb parts of the next frame, they slit the cell caps and waste honey. This angers the bees and you will have to put the inspection off for another time.

What You Need to Start

Empty frames are rectangular wooden frames that we can embed with wires at any time. Some beekeepers prefer these frames, because they allow bees to freely build their combs, so the beekeeper can just use a knife to cut the honeycombs whole.

Empty Frame   Wired Frame

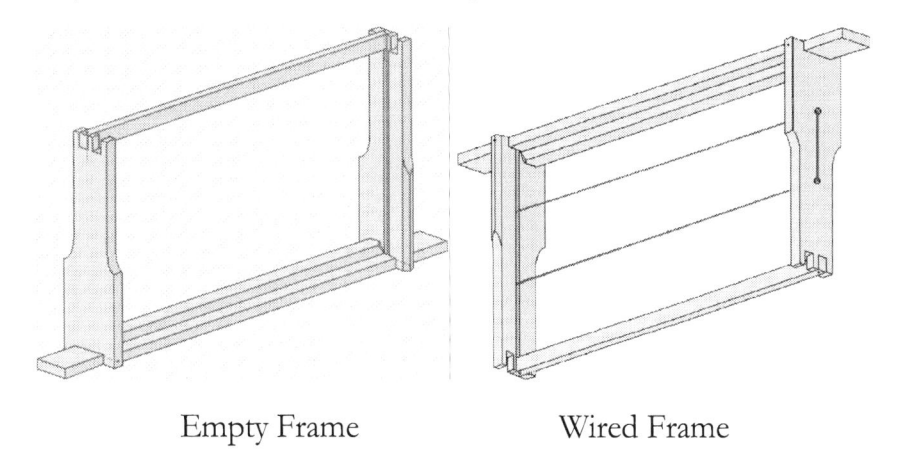

Photo courtesy: Dave Cushman

Wired frames are the most common ones. The number of wires depends on the size of your frame. The one shown above has two wires of a shallow or medium size. Deep frames usually have four wires because they are wider. The best thing about this kind of frame is its ability to hold and support honeycombs no matter the hive situation.

The frames normally have "V" convex starter wood/wax on the underside of the top bar. This helps the bees initiate wax building into combs.

A foundation frame has a molded plastic sheet of comb where bees can easily draw their cells outward. Before introducing bees into these frames, make sure that you garnish them with beeswax, otherwise the builder bees will not accept them. While this looks easier and faster, we personally do not recommend this to beginners, as you need a lot of time to study the behavior of your bees first.

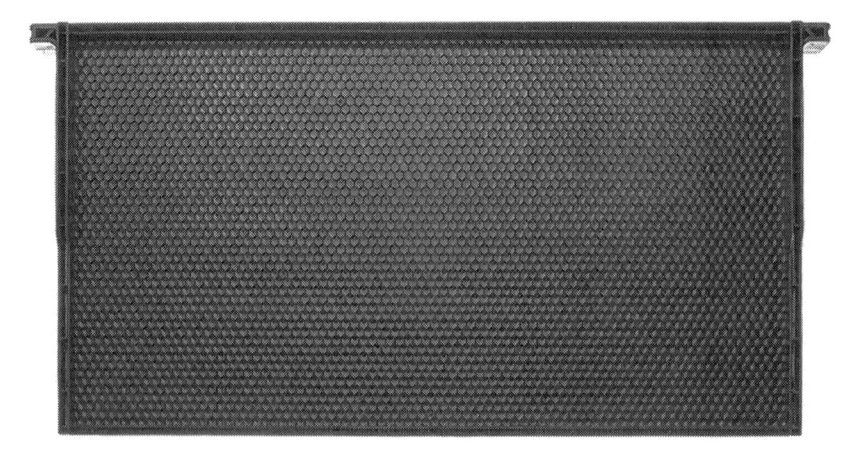

Foundation frame (Alibaba)

A newly manufactured plastic foundation may hinder pheromone communication between bees, which is a vital process in the colony. This type of frame can be recycled upon honey collection and may last for years compared to wooden frames, which may decay because of wood-eating microbes, or break from wear and tear. The pre-molded frame contains 3,500 cells. That means in a hive body of ten frames with two sides, you will have 70,000 cells for deep hive frames. This helps bees conserve energy from wax production and instead concentrate more on honey production. This ensures that the queen will always have cells to lay into as well.

Protective Suit

As a beginner, we expect you to wear protective gear for one simple reason: stings. Honeybee stings can be quite painful, and you will definitely get stung when working with bees. Unfortunately, bees die when they sting you, because they leave their stingers in you along with some vital parts of their bodies.

A complete protective gear has a coverall, veil, hat, and gloves.

A coverall is a suit that covers your whole body from ankle to neck. It has two layers of nylon or cotton. When I first tried on my coverall, it gave me a huge sense of confidence and security, which I needed for my first time working with bees. It does not always work, especially if you forget to cover all the openings on the wrists or ankles. You always need to bring tape with you to secure all those holes.

Coveralls with gloves, hat and veil

Coveralls can feel warm while working during the day. There are coveralls made of ventilated premium cotton, but they are pricier. These kinds have elastic and zippers around your ankles, wrists and waist. There are even coveralls with head covers attached. The veil and hat usually go together. Veils are see-through. Your veil should have its lower extension slipped inside the coverall to make sure no bees can enter the veil.

Just in case a bee slips in and finds its way onto your face, snap it as fast as you can. Do not give it a chance to sting any part of your face, especially your eye. One dead bee is better than going nearly or fully blind for the rest of your life.

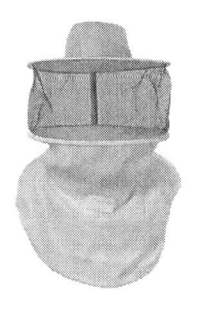

Veil & hat (GloryBee)   *Gloves (Flexzion)*   *Coverall (Flexzion)*

There are gloves made from goatskin and the usual plastic gloves we can buy at Walmart. In my own experience, it is quite difficult working with gloves on because you cannot fully grasp the feeling of what you are doing. When you handle frames with honey or brood, you need to be extra careful when moving your fingers to never drop it, or touch its sides or angles with capped cells.

The moment you drop a frame, it will cause an angry mob to attack you and everyone else in the area. Bees target hands the most when they become agitated, as the hands are what caused the disturbance to their hive.

Smoker

A smoker is an essential item for any beekeeper. Along with their own form of communication through pheromones, bees understand the language of smoke.

Wildfire indicates a threat to their hive. This phenomenon triggers bees to collect as much honey as they can to prepare for an emergency exit in case their combs are fully engulfed by fire.

Photo courtesy: Beebaltic

We only use smoke to cause a stir and shoo them away for a bit when working on the site. Too much smoke causes stress and excitement.

Always make sure to deliver a huge cloud of smoke in times of agitation, especially when there are people nearby or you are only wearing a hat and veil when commotion strikes.

Once you fill in the chamber with smoker fuel, light it up and squeeze the bellow to draw air in, igniting a fire to create smoke.

We collect the dried leaves of plants with wonderful scents in the summer to use as smoker fuel. Dead/dry leaves give off an aroma that bees do not like. You can use any materials to burn, including wood shavings, burlap, lavender leaves, sage, pine needles, and any organic materials in nature.

Hive Tools

Like any other person working in the field, a toolbox will always be with you wherever you go. There are many tools you should have; we will show you the four most used in the field.

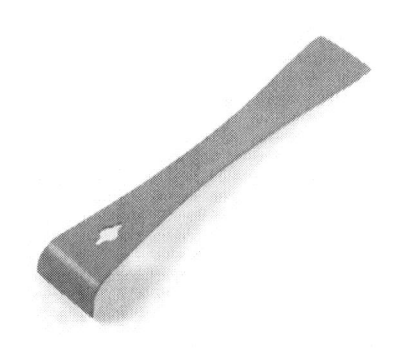

Standard hive tool. This has a flat end on one side and a half-crooked one on the other. Its flat end should be half-sharp because when you scrape away wax/propolis on the top bars, the surface can be oily, and it may cut you at the most unexpected moment. When you inspect your hives, you might see some burr combs, which are chunks of combs bees are starting to create where you do not want them to.

We use its crooked part to separate frames from one another. Others find it useless and tend to use the flat end instead. Always put extra care in separating one frame from another. When you remove a frame from its place in the hive, pull it up as slowly and gently as you can to give bees the time they need to scoot over.

J-hook tool. When you inspect each frame, you usually start from one side and work your way to the other side by removing the farthest frame off the box and sliding the others through. A J-hook is useful if you only need to check a frame or two in the middle. Insert the J-hook on one side of the frame, lift it up, do the same to the other end, then pull the whole frame through.

J-hooks should have pointed ends so that when you inspect capped cells and cut them open for signs of disease, you can use the pointed end to slice the capped cell open. You can use the sharp flat end as a scrapper as well.

Again, always be patient and careful when moving frames, especially the ones in the brood box. During bee inspection, a beekeeper should use minimal movements to avoid stressing the bees. Take care not to damage their delicate wings or squish them.

Uncapping fork. This is used to uncap (open) wax covering honey cells of the comb for honey harvesting. Some use a capping knife instead to open the cells. Unfortunately, this destroys the cell wax structures the bees will need to restructure the frames. We do not advise this, especially when you harvest honey before winter.

Bee brush. Instead of using the typical brush from Target, we personally recommend using a feather (because of its light bristles) when pushing bees aside as you work on a frame. Hard bristles flick and damage the wings.

You brush bees aside during inspection to get a clear picture of the status of the cells.

We will discuss other minor tools and materials later along with their uses.

Rules/Regulations

Every region, state, nation, etc. is different in its approach to beekeeping regulations. It is one's duty as a beekeeper to learn their local government's rules and regulations.

The United States congress passed the Honeybee Act of 1922 which restricts import of adult living honeybees into the US. With an amendment in 1976, pests and diseases were given consideration. The Secretary of the Department of Agriculture reinforced compliance of measures directed towards common pests and diseases of honeybees.

Your state's Department of Agriculture website details the process of licensing. Although not all states require a license, you still need to register your beekeeping practice for inspections (to monitor insects and diseases).

The Bee & Bee Caste

As complex social insects, honeybees are very adaptable to new enclosed areas. These days, it is difficult to find honeycombs in the open exposed to the physical environment. Unlike in nature, we keep them in man-made wooden hives that we buy or create and this is where the honeybees organize their caste system in the colony.

The bees' caste system has a complex structure which demands continuous movement for the survival of the whole colony. Now let us dive into the anatomy of a bee and discuss some of its general physiological processes which are relevant to beekeeping.

Bee Anatomy

The bee is probably the most important insect in the world. It is the most efficient pollinator of our crops. There are more than 16,000 species of bees but the honeybee (*Apis mellifera*) earned its name by being the only one capable of producing honey.

The honeybee has three main body parts: head, thorax and abdomen.

On its head, it has a pair of wide eyes, mouthparts and a pair of antennae; three pairs of legs and two pairs of wings on the thorax; and an abdomen with mostly black and yellow stripes around the stomach and bee blood (haemolymph).

Its compound eyes can see thousands of images per minute through UV light. An insect smells through their antennae and not through their breathing organ, which is on their abdomen. Bees have mandibles used to cut through food or other materials, and mold and cut cell wax.

The main way they collect nectar into their stomach is through their proboscis. The proboscis is like a tongue that elongates to reach the deeper parts of the nectaries housing nectar in the flower. Pollen sticks to bee hair. Honeybees usually use their hind legs to mash bags of pollen they carry back to the hive. Pollen is important for making beebread.

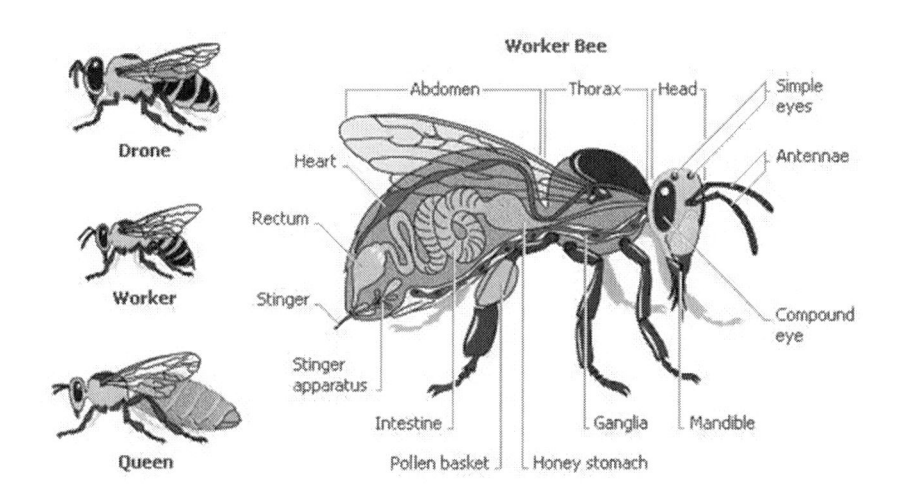

Bee Anatomy (Mahako)

Let us differentiate between honey, pollen and nectar. Honey is a semi-liquid product that bees produce from nectar. Nectar is a transparent sugary fluid used by the plant to attract pollinators such as bees. Pollen sticks to their bodies and they unknowingly bring it to another flower.

When bees mix honey with pollen, it becomes beebread. This is the actual food of the bees that produces energy, enabling their body to function and yield heat. The color of pollen depends on the flower the bee chooses to collect. Bees will only choose one kind of pollen to collect for the day.

Bees have glands all over their bodies where they produce secretions of compounds, substances, and pheromones. They mix the nectar they bring into the hive with these secretions. They then use enzymes to help synthesize nectar by vomiting it into another bee's stomach, and then another one, and so on until it is ready for fermentation inside the cell for honey capping. Capping is the process of covering young honey placed in a cell for fermentation to mature and become the sweet, sticky honey that we love to eat.

Let's run through the important glands of a honeybee:

1. Nasanov gland- found on the upper hind abdomen; secretes pheromones to help orient bees looking for food
2. Koschenikov gland- found on the lower hind abdomen; secretes alarm pheromone
3. Dufour's gland- found on the lower hind abdomen; marks eggs differentiating between ones laid by a queen and by a worker bee (unfertilized eggs)
4. Mandibular gland- located on the head below the mandibles; produces the royal jelly
5. Wax gland- located on the lower abdomen; produces wax for drawing comb

Other glands are used for pheromone production. Bee communication relies entirely on pheromones.

Pheromones

Pheromones are the vital messages transmitted within the colony. Each caste and age will have its own specific pheromones it produces. They tell bees when and how to initiate their tasks. This system makes bees one of the most uniquely coordinated insects in nature.

Bee communication is ineffective if there is a problem with the receiver or sender, the communication channel, or the message itself.

One of the reasons scientists around the world are so worried about climate change is that the increase in global temperature will disrupt bee communication. Heat can destabilize a compound or create a new one. When it affects the unique chemical structure of the pheromone, it weakens the compound, which causes bees send the wrong messages, or transmit no message at all.

The Queen Mandibular Pheromone (QMP) is the pheromone that regulates the whole colony's work. It also acts as a sex pheromone. QMP attracts the drones. If the drones don't recognize her scent, they will not be able to deposit their sperm. She is only viable for as long as thirty minutes. If you are wondering why there are no eggs being laid during mating season, the drones might not have been able to find the queen.

Worker bees send out two types of alarm pheromones; one is for defense and the other is a repellant to deter potential enemies. When you inspect a hive, some bees send these alarm pheromones, but if you use a smoker, the smoke masks the pheromone signal.

Bee Caste

The honeybee caste system is composed of three adults: workers, drones, and a queen. Workers are all female bees that do not lay fertilized eggs. Drones are all male bees. The queen is the head of the hive and the only fertile female bee. All bees undergo the same developmental stages from egg to adulthood. Each caste has its own distinct role to play in the hive.

Queen: Egg (3 days), Larva (8 ½ days), Capped (7 ½ days), Pupa (8 days)

Worker: Egg (3 days), Larva (9 days), Capped (9 days), Pupa (10/11 days)

Drone: Egg (3 days), Larva (9 ½ days), Capped (10 ½ days), Pupa (10 days)

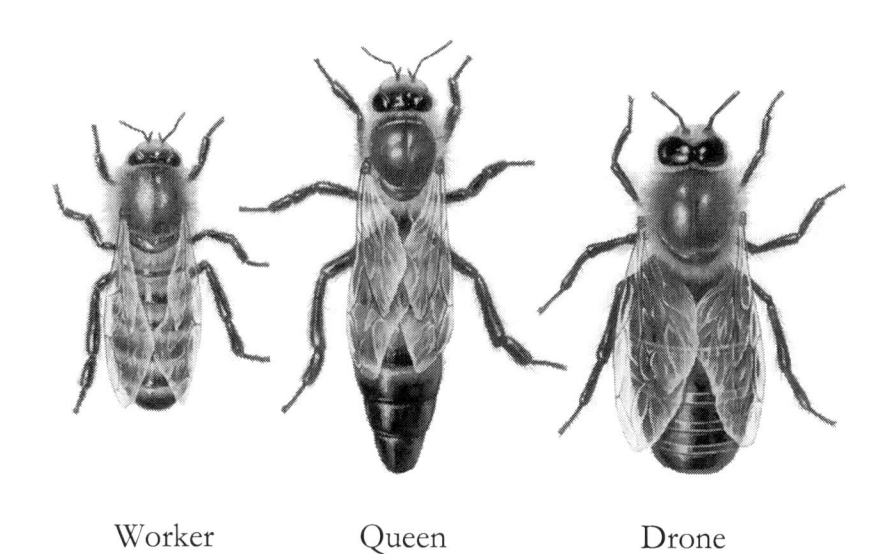

Worker · Queen · Drone

Three major castes (Liupalmer)

Rearing is the process of bringing up the egg into a larva, and the larva to a pupa, until the young bee can fulfill its responsibility in the hive. Each caste has its own developmental stages with different nutritional requirements in its larval state.

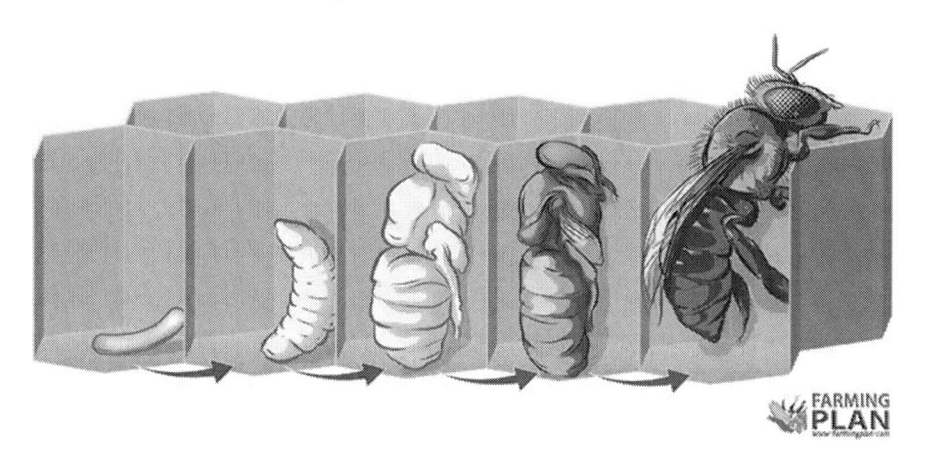

Egg   Larva   Pupa   Adult

Life stages of a Honeybee (FarmingPlan)

The life of a bee starts with being an egg. Then it develops into a larva, which is an immature stage of an insect that looks like a worm. The larva undergoes the pupal stage, wherein the immature organism becomes inactive inside a cocoon. It transforms itself inside and emerges as a young adult bee.

As a new beekeeper, it's important to learn the differences in the physical appearance of the castes in the hive. Each caste cannot survive without the others. Like any other living organism, it is instinctual for bees to live just to proliferate. We might never know if bees comprehend their significance to humans, but it is enough for us to be thankful for what they do for us.

Queen

A **queen** is responsible for reproducing fertilized (female) and unfertilized (male) eggs in the colony that become workers, drones and even new queens. She is the only fertile female bee in the hive and delegates most of the activities in the colony using her communicative pheromone (QMP). This makes her the most important bee in the hive.

She starts as a fertilized female egg laid on a special brood cell called a queen cup. This cylindrical cup protrudes out of the uniform waxed cells. She then becomes a larva and swims in royal jelly mixed with water.

The larval stage is the identifying stage for all female bees. All larvae eat both honey and royal jelly; however, a queen larva eats royal jelly alone. This jelly further distinguishes her physiological development and helps her to become a bee capable of laying fertilized and unfertilized eggs.

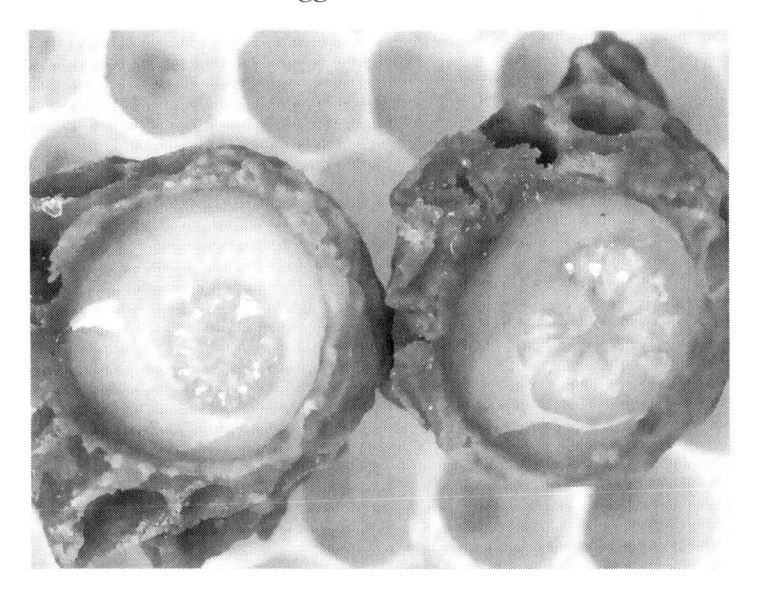

Honey and other materials limit other female bees' fertility.

The queen bee emerges into adulthood 16 days after the previous queen lays her in her queen cell. She then eliminates other young queen candidates to earn the crown. You can easily identify a queen bee by her physical appearance. Her body is longer and more slender than the others, and her wings cover about two thirds of her abdomen whereas the wings of both workers and drones reach the tips.

Because she is bigger than the other female bees, she cannot pass through the queen excluder, designed to accommodate worker bees alone.

She starts mating a week after emerging. She flies out of the hive followed by several drones smelling her scent, usually in the afternoon. Her spermatheca will receive three to eight billion sperm, and that is all she needs to lay fertilized eggs.

She is capable of laying 1,000 to 1,500 eggs a day, especially in the peak season, which is spring and summer. The average lifespan of a bee is around 21 days. If she dies, egg laying will come to a halt and the colony will need to replace her right away.

By the time the queen grows old and ceases to lay eggs, workers will rear a new queen in her place.

The process of replacing a queen with her own daughter is called supersedure. This process can be natural or initiated depending on the circumstances.

Decades ago, scientists thought that bee workers choose a potential queen by excessively feeding her with royal jelly to help develop the functional female reproductive organs. Only recently in 2015, it was discovered that NOT feeding the immature candidate any pollen or honey is actually the secret formula for making a queen bee.

Her queen mandibular pheromone is the most important message that conveys different signals depending on what she thinks the hive needs. This is why she is called the queen; the hive is not just dysfunctional, but lifeless without her.

When you finally establish your first hive, you need to find the queen first and mark her using neon-colored pen on her back thorax between her wings. This will help you identify her when inspecting your hives.

Drones

A **drone** is a male bee primarily focused on mating with the queen to ensure genetic propagation. Drones are unfertilized eggs that stay in the brood cells longer than workers do. Their cells have blunt, concave-like bullets that protrude compared to worker cells that are flat. This is one way for you to distinguish between worker and drone cells early in their pupal stage.

The queen decides how many eggs to lay in the hive. Worker bees can also lay eggs but they will only hatch into drones since they are unfertilized. Drones do not simply mate and eat honey; they have a certain role in the hive that beekeepers and scientists do not exactly understand.

It is not their function to protect the hive from other bees or insects; workers do that. In fact, drones can willingly visit any hive they want, dally up with a virgin queen and eat the other hive's honey, and sometimes do so. They sometimes gather with drones from other hives, as if they are having a meeting. There are many theories, but no one really knows what they are doing.

Drones do not sting. When they mate with a queen, their sexual organ falls off, along with associated abdominal tissues, which results in their death. In the fall when food is scarce and honey diminishes, workers force drones to leave the hive to ensure steady supply of honey for the brood. They are ruthlessly left to die out in the cold winter.

Workers

All **workers** are female honeybees. They are the backbone of the hive. In their larval stage, adult workers feed them beebread instead of just royal jelly. Beebread undergoes fermentation after mixing with honey. Workers are the smallest in the hive, yet make up most of the colony and do most of the work. Worker bees start working right when they emerge from the egg.

Let's discuss the life cycle of the worker bee:

1. On days 1 and 2 after emerging from the egg, young worker bees clean the brood cells to ready them for the next use. A cleaner bee must meticulously clean a cell for a queen bee to lay an egg in it. If not properly done, the queen scouts another cell and workers need to clean that cell again.

2. From days 3 to 11, they become nurse bees. These nurses start feeding worker and drone larvae with royal jelly at day 1 and 2 after egg hatching. Later, these nurse bees feed them with pollen mixed water and other micronutrients until they pupate. We also have what we call advanced nurse bees. The task of these bees is to feed royal jelly to the queen larva, and never add any other nutrient composition.

3. Days 12 to 17 are for wax production. These almost adult worker bees build cells and repair damaged ones using wax. At the same time, they are to store pollen and honey which was foraged from outside the hive by older worker bees.

4. From days 12 to 16 and beyond, worker bees are free to choose which type of job they want to do in the hive. There are specific groups that will work on specific tasks and there are groups who will work on all or most activities inside the hive.

Now, we'll discuss some of the tasks of the worker bees:

a. Foraging. Foragers scout the area for pollen and nectars with which to produce honey. Bees use their proboscis to suck nectar from flowers. They go about five miles in any direction to sip nectar and collect pollen. Some workers pick resinous materials (from tree buds and plant/insect saps) at a certain time of day to produce propolis. Propolis is a sticky substance the worker bees use for various reasons that mainly acts as a glue. Foragers travel in groups into the flora every morning or at a time of the day when the flowers are at full bloom.

Some groups fetch water. When water is scarce during summer, you may see bees fly into your house, especially the kitchen where water is available. This is an indication that your water trough is dry and you need to refill it.

b. Orientation flight. A bee needs to learn how to navigate through your area to forage. She learns this from a bee scout whose job is to look for potential sources of food. The scout bee dances in front of the others to show them how and where she found the food source.

If food is within 50 to 150 meters, the bee scout goes back to the hive and dances in circles. Beyond that, she waggles back and forth in a straight line while vibrating her wings. She repeats this following the figure "8". If she walks straight following a line, the direction indicates where the sun is. If she waggles to the right, the direction is right facing the sun. If left, the direction is to the left facing the sun.

c. Propolizing. This is the process of creating and secreting propolis. Propolis is the bee glue that is made by honeybees by mixing saliva with wax and is used to seal any unwanted openings in the hive or to conceal it from foreign entities that pose a threat to it. Some beekeepers do not like when bees propolize spaces such as between the covers, frames and sides of the body. It causes difficulty in opening the hive and separating one frame from another.

If you are not careful when opening the hive and you exert too much force when separating covers, you can tip the hive over, which we mistakenly did once. It did not go well. However distracting, propolizing is important in maintaining temperature within the hive. The more holes are covered, the more heat-regulated the hive is during winter. If there is a decaying body too big to be dragged outside, they propolize the cadaver to limit its infectious potential.

d. Cleaning. A worker cleans the hive regularly. She removes dead bees and aborted larvae to ensure no microbes can thrive and cause diseases in the hive. Bees are very strict with cleanliness; when you inspect their hives, you will never see a spec of dirt inside, unless they are sick.

When the comb is brooded three to five times, it becomes dark to black because of the pupal cocoon left inside. It is best to have it replaced to make sure pathogens are not lurking for any chance to strike.

e. Sealing. Honey sealers play a crucial part in honey making. A bee should know exactly when to seal a cell with honey materials. Honey must mature, becoming sufficiently dry and sticky before sealing. If it is a bit wet, they need to dry it by fanning it with their wings. When bees need honey as food, they chew the cap away and eat what is inside.

f. Feeding. Worker bees feed everyone in the colony, except mature drones. Drone larvae are an exception. Worker bees continue to bring royal jelly to the queen even when mature. At the same time, the bees that are looking out for the queen help spread out QMP by fanning the hive.

g. Nursing. Brood rearing is the task of nurse bees. In 3 to 4 days, the workers will deliver food to the larvae depending on their needs. Later on, they seal the cells for the pupal stage. The nurse bees smell the pheromone secreted by a larva so they know if they are working on a worker, drone or queen cell.

h. Building. Other worker bees draw the comb using wax provided by wax-producing workers (young adult bees). Building combs takes a lot of energy and wax material. If bees are not able to build comb around late summer, give extra attention to that hive during winterization.

i. Guarding. Guard bees watch the entrance of the hive for intruders such as wasps, other insects and rodents. They inspect everything that comes into the hive - even foragers bringing in pollen - by smelling it. A guard bee will show a defensive posture by standing on her four hind legs. She holds her antennae straight up to assess the situation, and if it is too much to handle, she excites the alarm pheromone for backup. Help always comes in a matter of seconds and everyone attacks the intruder.

j. Robbing. Bees also rob other hives, mainly to secure honey. It can happen at any time and is a serious problem in autumn, but it can be manageable. Stronger colonies prey on weaker hives, especially if they are dysfunctional. This is natural for bees. If your location has few nectar sources, stronger colonies will steal food from other hives.

Once, we mistakenly added a weak super with frames half-filled with honey hoping for the original colony to accept them. Within hours, robbing happened, and the super was honey-emptied in a flash. Many bees from both colonies died. You should keep in mind that worker bees do not always accept bees from other hives.

The activities in the hive depend on the quality of pheromone the queen sends off to the colony. The status of the queen determines the status of your hive. However, it is the workers who decide who the queen will be, if she is a good fit for the hive or if she needs to be replaced. All bees in the colony work hand in hand for the sake of proliferation.

The Brood

The egg looks like a tiny grain of white rice. When the queen deposits the egg into a cell, it stands straight up for three days. If you want to see the eggs, hold the frame up against the sun and you will notice a silhouette of grain-like objects inside. The queen starts the brood in the middle and works her way outward. This is what we call the laying pattern and it will have different implications in terms of beehive management.

The brood box can be single or double. You double the brood box by adding another deep super and frames for bees to work on. If you have newer supers added on top of the main body, these usually have lighter combs because only honey is stored inside, whereas the frame combs in the main body are darker since they have been brooded a few times. It will be harder to look for eggs in darker combs. We usually clean the frames every four or five years.

From an egg, the bee develops into a grub, which begins the larval phase.

Five nursing bees feed each larva a hundred times a day for an average of six days for worker and drone larvae. They curl like the letter "C," swimming in bee milk, water and honey. After six days, the adult workers cap their cells, and inside, the larva spins its cocoon preparing for the pupal stage.

The pupal stage for new workers is 12 days, 14 ½ for drones, and 7 ½ for new queens. Within these days, the pupa begins to take the form of an adult starting with the color of its eyes, from white to brown or purple. The whole body follows, emerging from the cell and starting to clean itself. Then it's off to work as a young full-fledged bee.

Establishment & Management

We highly recommend that you start beekeeping in spring (May/April) or early summer since that is when the bees will be working hard to build their hive. Starting in spring will help you understand your bees more. Like any other living organism, winter is a harsh season for bees. As beekeepers, it is our duty to intervene in situations bees cannot manage themselves so they can store enough honey when there is not enough food from the field.

By now, you should already have a few notes to keep in mind for when you buy your first beehive colony. If you decide to transfer bees into your first permanent hive box, spring will help bees easily fill those combs with honey for winter. Before you write that check, be sure to familiarize yourself with the dos and don'ts of beekeeping and its management.

Establishment

Once you've chosen a location, you are ready to set up your first hive. Nowadays, new beekeepers usually buy established or nuc hives to start their first colonies. Either way, we highly recommend you have at least two or three capped brood frames (complete with all castes), a frame of honey, and a free/empty frame. Make sure that all cells for the first three frames are full with brood and honey.

The day you buy the hive, open the entrance so the bees can familiarize themselves with the new area. If you decided to transfer the frames into the new empty hive you bought, make sure the size of the frames and the size of the empty boxes you have are the same.

If the queen is unmarked, mark her right away for easy inspection. Some beekeepers grab the queen by the wings and use the other hand to hold her body with their pointer and thumb fingers, but we personally do not do this as there was a time when we accidentally tore a queen bee's wing and she died the day after. You can use a marking cage (screen) which presses the queen and keeps her still so you can mark her from that confined position.

Once established, make sure the queen is settling in well and laying eggs. Check their food supply, and if they are starting to draw wax cells. Do this inspection a week after setting up the new hive.

Management (Seasonal)

Say you decided to preorder your colony before January and visit the beekeeper around February or March. Old worker bees from the winter season recede during these months and they are rearing the brood as best as they can to prepare new workers for spring. The more brood cells you have, the stronger your colony will be.

If you can acquire the colony earlier in January, this is better. They have a greater chance to swarm in spring and you can start a new colony in a second empty hive box if you opted to buy one. It is your choice if you want to transfer the frames from the nuc colony you bought into your new permanent hive box right away or wait until April. A nuc hive box is good for reproducing new colonies, but not for permanent hiving as it is small and bees will do things that new beekeepers will have a difficult time comprehending.

Spring and Summer

Bees are everywhere during these two seasons. Some hives come out of winter strong, some weak. Others die because of robbing or because the autumn preparation for winterization was not effective enough.

In the spring, the queen lays the most eggs, and that number climbs until the summer solstice and then decreases. If you do not see any eggs or brood in the summer, your hive is in trouble. Bees cannot survive with a body temperature above 100°F, so water should always be available to help ventilate and cool the hive in the summer.

Post-Winter/Pre-Spring

Pre-spring activities start with inspecting what has transpired over the winter and determining whether your hives are ready for spring and summer operations, which are hectic. You remove the insulation cover you placed last fall. We normally check the removable lower boards of the hive to see how many died over the winter. This will also help us check if there is mold growing inside. From here, we will learn whether we can introduce the weak hive to another one.

Feeding

Feeding means giving bees an alternative source of food in case their natural food source does not fit their taste buds or if food is far away. You do this right away when you start beekeeping. We no longer feed our bees in the spring, but some parts of the state still do because their spring comes late. You can either feed bees with liquid or dry sugar.

For solid sugar, you directly place a piece of thick paper on top of the top-bar frames just below the inner cover and place the dry sugar on it. Do not cover the entire top surface so bees can have space to move freely. Add an extra shallow body to provide space for the sugar before adding the inner and outer cover.

For sugar syrup, we formulate feed at different ratios. In spring, it is a 1:1 ratio, which means equal parts water and sugar. Some beekeepers add other nutritional content to their feed in smaller quantities. Feeding provides bees with the carbohydrate and protein source they need. This will take a chunk of your investment, especially if your flora is not naturally rich.

Honey-sellers use feeding methods to promote honey production for business. Honey made from artificial food sources is cheaper because it has lower quality than honey from a flower's nectar.

Let's discuss the various types of feeders:

1. **Entrance feeders.** These vary in size and have a jar hole in the middle. This middle hole supports the lid of a mason jar. The lid will have small holes where bees can access the feed. You slip the jar upside down into the hole. Bees can directly travel into the feeder from inside the hive.

2. **Frame feeders.** You can hang a frame feeder together with an actual frame. This has an open slot on the top bar where you can pour the feed inside.

3. **Open-air feeder.** This is any container holding feed and placed far enough away to limit robbing from nearby hives.

4. **Top feeders.** Top feeders fit your hive like a body. It is like another body but with a bottom board. You transfer the feed into this top container and bees can come from the middle slot entrance. You need to add floaters for bees to land on. You add the inner cover on top and then the outer. These feeders decrease robbing.

5. **Rapid feeder.** This one is smaller and fits inside a nuc hive. You fill it with feed and the bees eat the syrup from the middle through the edge from underneath.

6. **Pail feeder.** In the middle of the pail lid is a hole with screen. You fill the pail with feed and place it over the top of the hole in the inner cover. This is good since bees will not need to leave the hive and can just go straight up the inner cover where feed is coming from. You can cover the pail with an empty hive body and then place the outer cover.

We add floaters to all feeders (except the rapid feeder designed to inhibit drowning) so bees have something to land on and they don't drown.

Types of feed vary from one state to another. Protein source is not really an issue but carbohydrate source can be. Carbohydrates become the energy that bees use to draw out heat to fight the cold in the winter.

Inspection

Inspection will also vary from one season to another. Always keep in mind that every time you do this, you are disturbing the hive. You should be very careful and observant of what is going on before and after every inspection.

These are your initial steps every time you do inspection:

1. Check the outside situation of the hive. Check if bees are acting strange, check for the presence of dead bees, and note whether foragers are flying in and out, as they should.

Establishment & Management

2. Open the top cover and set it aside leaning against the sun or set it on the ground with the underside facing up.

3. Puff in some light smoke on top.

4. Slowly remove the inner cover and puff in some smoke again.

5. Start with the frame on the farthest side (any side) and work your way up to the opposite side.

6. As you go from one frame to another, always be on the lookout for the queen. If she is in that frame, leave it for a while and come back to it later.

Open the top covers slowly to avoid shocking the hive with full sunlight. Check the hive first for unwanted insects and get rid of them right away. Also, check the stage of the brood by checking the cells to see if there are eggs that were recently laid. Check to see the laying pattern of the queen. Queens normally start to lay eggs in the middle of the frame and move outward.

Brood boxes are not uniform in cells. There will be frames that have worker cells, or drone cells, or a combination of brood and honey, or even beebread and pollen.

After a quick inspection, always be careful when setting the boxes back on top of each other since it can crush bees running on top of the main body. This does not always happen but if it does, they propolize the cadaver and it will be hard for you to do your next inspection when the boxes stick to one another.

Cnidophobia

Cnidophobia is the fear of being stung by something. Being stung is something that happens to all beekeepers, no matter how careful they are. If you do not know if you're allergic to bee stings, the only way to find out is to visit a doctor. The physician will inject a small amount of allergen extract into the skin of your arm or upper back. If redness, swelling, or a painful reaction occur, you are allergic.

What do you do after being stung?

Remove the stinger using tweezers or by swiping a flat card against it. Then find the nearest source of soap and water and wash the affected area. Apply a cold compress. If the pain persists, you can take pain relievers. Buy a hydrocortisone cream or calamine lotion to ease the swelling. Never, ever scratch the area.

You can overcome cnidiphobia and become more confident by spending time with your bees. Honeybees are not naturally aggressive; they only sting to protect their hives. If you work carefully and not disturb them too much, your bees will love you back. Remember to always keep your bee toolbox, containing medicine and cream, with you.

Supering

Supering is adding/removing supers on the hive depending on the performance of the bees drawing combs. Use your judgment to super the hives when needed. Oversupering means adding supers (usually in the summer) while undersupering means removing supers (usually in the winter).

Check the population of the brood box. If the population is excessive, you can add a deep box and a shallow one on top of it. If you see honey dripping everywhere, it means the hive population is crowded.

When supering, you always need to transfer some honey frames from the main box into the new, empty super. You place the empty frames into the brood box as a replacement for the frame combs you will place into the new super. This process will help the bee workers easily draw comb in the empty frames from both the old and new bodies.

If the workers are drawing comb and adding honey quickly, you can add medium or shallow boxes in a week or so following the same transfer process. However, frame sizes will no longer be the same, so you no longer need to exchange frames. This is where you source honey, as this is the surplus food of the colony.

Supering is not only limited to spring; you can oversuper as needed. Bear in mind that the honey you harvest depends on the quantity of nectar in the area and the budget you have for artificial feeding.

Supersedure

Superseding is the process of replacing the queen bee with a new virgin queen for various reasons, including the queen suddenly dying, producing fewer eggs, producing weaker pheromones, or getting sick.

Sometimes the workers decide to supersede the queen on their own terms. You might believe that the current queen is still healthy, but the workers think otherwise.

This process does not produce a new hive or colony, unlike swarming. Natural supersedure happens in late summer or early fall. If the workers smell the declining pheromone strength of the queen, or if they get the hint that there is something wrong with her, they will replace her by starting to build new queen cells and nursing them right away.

You can initiate supersedure yourself. It does not always happen every year; queens may live up to five years naturally. Some beekeepers replace their queens every two or three years, especially if they want more workers to draw honey.

When we accidentally tore a queen bee's wings, the hive was confused for a day. In two weeks, we saw two new queen cups built in the fourth frame. These are what we call emergency queen cells. These cells may not always result in healthy, strong and prolific queens. They are nursed with the given quality of royal jelly available, which sometimes results in a weaker QMP and consequently a weaker hive.

Swarming

Swarming is the natural means of colony reproduction. It happens when there is not enough space in the hive because the colony is growing or there is not enough space to nurse brood. The old queen can swarm to another place, bringing with her almost 60% of the bee population. Prior to hatching new virgin queens, the old one must leave. She can take 20,000 to 30,000 bees with her from the original home.

The swarm flies through the air in the spring, which is both frightening and beautiful to watch at the same time. Later you will learn that swarms are more docile than television shows portray them as. In fact, you can catch swarms resting on tree branches with your bare hands!

Some of the bees scout to find a permanent home, which can take an hour to three days. When bees swarm to completely unfamiliar places it is hard for them to survive. With the threat of erratic climate patterns, bees rely hard on pheromones for communication.

Most of the time, these swarms only live for a year outside of the colony and die. That is why we developed the art of catching swarms! Beekeepers create a temporary hive and place it under the shade of trees but high enough from the ground that it's somewhere that bees would naturally nest. We wipe the frames inside with wax and honey to lure bees in and make them start drawing combs. Then we collect the frames and transfer them into permanent hives.

We can also prevent and control swarming. Keep the hive properly ventilated in the summer and check the number of bees per hive. If workers start to build queen cups, but the queen is still in perfect health, remove all these swarm cells to postpone swarming.

We can also bait swarms in two ways: First, cut a chunk of old comb and hang it somewhere. Bees will be swarming in it in no time. There are many pheromone luring traps for bees to settle into, but they do not always work. The second way is to remove a combed frame and place it on another hive with empty frames. We use that as bait for swarms just in case. We either create a new hive, or place that on top of the single brood box.

Some beekeepers do not want swarming as production of honey recedes and those who produce new queens can lose the original queen. For prevention, we label which colony is a candidate for swarming.

Splitting

You can split a hive once you have mastered your practice in order to replace losses or keep bee population uncongested in the hive. This is best if bees come out strong from the winter. Aside from catching swarms, splitting is the best way to increase the number of your colonies.

Let's discuss two effective ways to split a hive.

First, find the queen from a large colony and cage her for safety. Inspect the hive to determine whether it is indeed a candidate for splitting. You know it is a strong one if there's too much honey produced and more bees are flying over the hive compared to others.

In addition, when opening the hive, you can no longer see much space between frames, and there are queen cells present.

Check the brood box by working through it frame by frame. In your new empty hive of the same size has the same number of empty frames, take four out. These empty frames will replace the old ones from the strong hive we are splitting. From this strong hive, we take three capped brood frames and place them into the new split hive. We place these frames in the middle of the second deep box, not on its sides. The fourth frame should have honey in it. Now, transfer some bees into this new split by shaking bees from the old hive. The bees that stay in the new split hive are usually nurse bees, who will rear the eggs the old queen will soon lay. Get your caged queen and introduce her to the new split hive.

Place the four empty frames into the middle of the old box. This method is technically following a swarming situation but you are the one initiating the process. Most likely, a supersedure will follow in the old hive. New brood will hatch quickly, producing new workers for the split hive. If you are doing this in the spring, the new hive will rear younger bees.

If you do not have that much space in your site, you can reduce the size of your entrance (new split hive) to limit bees from foraging in the first week and going back to the old colony.

The second technique is literally splitting a big hive (a double-hive). You can do this by adding a new brood box on top of the first one.

In a deep box with empty frames, you take four out, replace four brood frames from the first brood box, and place them on the second box. Shake some bees from four frames of the old box into the second box and place it on top. The bees will repopulate the second box and draw comb, new workers will arise, and in three days, you can separate this brood box into another area in the hive as the main body of a new colony. Most likely, this new hive will requeen for the new hive colony, or if you decided to follow a requeening process, you can introduce one into the new hive.

Autumn and Winter

This is a great time of year to start beekeeping and studying your hives. The goal of autumn activities is to prepare for the winter. During this time, you need to make sure the bees are ready for winterization, especially if your area experiences extreme winters. Remarkably, worker bees can live for four to six months in the winter compared to just a few weeks in the spring or summer, given that the queen is doing her part in secreting strong QMP to let the hive know she is still healthy.

The best way to determine if the queen is still there is by finding eggs. Eggs can only stay as they are for three days, so if you see one, then the queen was there recently. However, the queen will undergo a rest period and refrain from laying eggs over the winter. She will resume in the spring.

Around September, cover your hive with an insulator. Any will do as long as it does not cover your entrance and ventilation. You can buy beehive insulators online made out of foam or use old cardboard boxes from packages you can customize to cover your hives.

Make sure that your main entrance is free from ice and snow to allow ventilation. Another thing you need to add is a moisture board placed in between the inner and outer cover. Moisture condenses and becomes ice-cold water, which can cause hypothermia. During the winter, the bees' body temperature cannot go below 41°F, or they will die. Bees can no longer fly at temperatures lower than 55°F or higher than 100°F.

Autumn is also a time for feeding. Not all bees will accept different kinds of feeding strategies. By late August or September, you should have already experimented with artificial food and learned which feeding strategies the bees are likely to accept.

Autumn Feeding

One way to know how much more food the hive needs for the winter is to weigh each body. If the main brood is around 70 to 80 pounds, we normally want the hive to gain more pounds of honey until it's over 100. This way, we can make sure the hive will have enough or more than enough food to get through the winter.

Depending on which type of feed you use, you can add a whole bag of sugar or add autumn syrup in a ratio of 2:1. For autumn feeding, we normally start around early September and check the hive once a month, giving them another batch of food only if there is nothing left.

Robbing

Robbing is a common situation in beehives, especially during feeding time. If the weak bees cannot fully protect themselves, they will lose all their honey storage and die before winter ends. Some new beekeepers might mistakenly believe the death of the hive to have been caused by diseases. However, signs and symptoms will tell us otherwise.

Robbing always happens if there is not enough food. It will be hard for you to start if this is the case, because we do not want to constantly feed our bees with artificial food; we want them to convert nature's secret ingredient into honey. If you are starting with a hive with two or three bodies, bees will not be able to rob other hives because you only have one colony.

Pests and Diseases

Pests and diseases are always a threat to the normal and healthy functioning of any living organism. Many insects, mites and diseases endlessly threaten our bees. We will discuss the most common ones in America.

Varroa mites are a huge problem across the world for honeybees. There are other parasitic mites but varroa destructors are not named as such for nothing. We have diseases such as American Foulbrood (AFB) and European Foulbrood (EFB) for the brood, and Nosema for adult bees.

You should be able to diagnose such occurrences in the hive. If diagnosis is difficult, you can call your state bee inspector. If you have identified the presence of mites and diseases in your hive, you are required to report it to the bee inspector immediately.

Mites

Mites are the biggest pest problem for honeybees. The mites' parasitic behavior on bees of any caste can result in the colony's death. The mite is big enough for you to see. It is round, brown, orange or reddish in color, and about the size of a nail head.

Varroa female mites lay eggs inside the cell just before the bees cap it for larvae to pupate. Mites slip into the drone cells and wait for the workers to cap it. The mite then tears into the cocoon and feasts on the larva's haemolymph. In three days, it starts to lay male eggs and then females as well. These little mites mature and mate with each other. When the drone bee emerges from the cocoon, the other mites cling to other bees, thus continuing a cycle of infestation.

These mites cling to the bee's hair just like lice that infect humans. Once clung to the bee's body, they start feeding off its blood. That is why even when bees fly fast, mites are hard to get rid of, unless the bees purposely scratch their bodies.

Beekeepers use powder to sprinkle on bees so that they clean themselves and scratch mites away. Through IPM methods, these mites fall onto the sticky floor and become stuck.

This is an important strategy in IPM as counting the population of mites can help the inspector assess the extent of the situation so he or she knows how much pesticide should be applied.

American Foulbrood

AFB is an incurable bacterium and destruction by fire is the only way to manage it. It is the most widespread and contagious of bee diseases. It infects the larva and kills it when it becomes a pupa.

During inspection, shake the bees off and inspect one frame. If you see that the worker bees' pattern of capping brood is not uniform, wherein some cappings are empty, some have dead pupae, others are chewed with little holes, and some cells are mostly dark, it means they are infected with AFB. When you poke a matchstick inside the sunken darker cell, you will see a slimy, greasy consistency with a strong foul odor.

In a severe case of AFB, the cells are uncapped and scales are present inside the cells. When you check the frame, tilt it so you can see the bottom of the cell where the dead larva is likely to lay. It will not be on the curved end of the cell because remember, the bee draws the cell outward and not upward. The bottom of the cell is not the base, but the lower part parallel to the ground surface.

AFB is transmitted through infected food, an infected hive, stagnant water and equipment. Within 24 hours of infection, it will spread through the hive. We manage infected hives by burning them because the bacterium can stay viable for decades, even if it is in an early stage and only some exhibit symptoms.

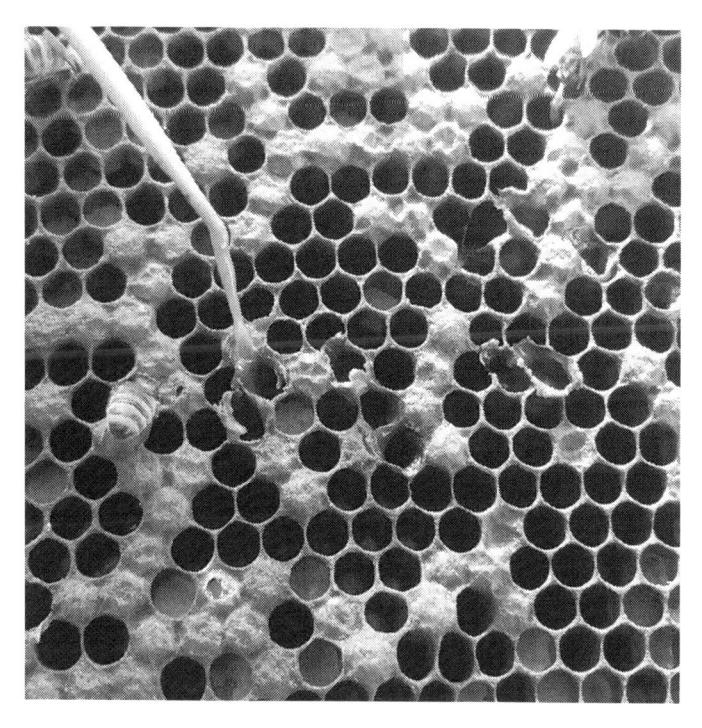

It is possible to sterilize the hive but protocol is to burn the hives with the bees. Foundation frames will melt when steam sterilized. You can sterilize your tools by heating them at high temperatures or soaking them in ten percent chlorine solution (bleach) for ten minutes. You can buy this chlorine solution from any department store.

European Foulbrood

Early symptoms of European foulbrood may look like AFB but they differ in many ways. Drone brood often show the first symptoms of EFB. The larva's color will change from white to yellow and then to yellowish brown.

An infected larva coils on the side of the cell in four to five days, not glistening nor pearly white. It twists before reaching pupal stage, then dries in two to four weeks.

It does not persist that much because of how the bacterium reproduces, which is good. However, it is important to differentiate AFB from EFB as burning may not be suggested for EFB since antibiotics can be used. Inspection for this disease is in spring and autumn.

Nosema

Nosema is a gut disease that builds up in a large population. It usually occurs around autumn and winter. It is a fungus that spreads through fecal matter and causes diarrhea. One symptom of nosema is fecal staining on the hive. Most hives are white, so we can see yellow to brown feces squirted on the hive or nearby, which indicates nosema.

The best way to diagnose nosema is to collect older bees dying on the ground defecating. Once collected, send them to the state apiary laboratory you can contact through your local government office.

Remember: the control and management of these diseases will depend on the decision of the apiary officer. They will send samples of dead bees or signs gathered from the hive to a lab specialist and make a recommendation from there.

Every location has different diseases and pests, which is why we encourage you to always be on the lookout for irregularities and abnormal behaviors from your bees. Check for minor insects such as small hive beetles and wax moths that are roaming around your bees.

Honey and Beeswax

Honey Properties

We harvest honey around late July through August. Tenured beekeepers harvest their honey two or three times a year. The good thing about honey is that it does not spoil. Yes, it can stay viable for decades.

The natural antifungal and antibacterial properties of honey keep its shelf life almost eternal. Though healthy honey is an almost perfect food, it may not be edible when infected with disease. Once disease is present in a frame, we postpone honey harvesting for that hive.

So how do adult bees process honey?

Photo courtesy: Beebaltic

They start by sipping nectar into their stomachs and on their way to the hive, their digestive system adds enzymes to it, resulting in a product called young honey.

This processed young honey will need to be regurgitated into another bee's stomach and then another to fully pack it with nutrients so it can become a simple sugar. Finally, the last bee can deposit the watery honey into the cells for fermentation. Then they seal it with wax. The enzymes from the bees' stomachs mixed with the nectar will intensify the fermentation process and when ready, it becomes honey.

The color of your honey depends on the diet of your bees. Mainly, the plant species available in your area will determine the honey spectrum and may vary along with the seasonal flower of the year.

Remember that if you want to brand your honey for commercial purposes as organic, the local Department of Agriculture officer who will approve your business permit will ask the bee inspector to check the area within five to ten miles to make sure there are no nearby farms using inorganic pesticides.

Harvest and Storage

Honey has natural antibacterial and antifungal properties. Once we filter the impurities out of honey, it will last indefinitely on its own when stored in a glass container. This is how we harvest our honey:

1. Inspect the hive, checking each space between frames to see if honey is drawn and waxed. Draw a frame out and check if at least 95 percent or more on both sides are fully wax closed/

capped. Do not collect uncapped honey, as it is not ready. It will only spoil your product.

2. Smoke or brush the bees out. Place the honey frame into a container or an empty body you can easily transport from the site to your house. Never draw out honey on the site to keep bees from coming and sipping honey back in.

3. Uncap the frames using an uncapping knife and place in the honey extractor.

4. Spin the extractor manually or if electric, follow the instructions in the manual.

5. Use a strainer to remove unwanted solid particles such as cell wax or any foreign material finding its way in.

6. Transfer into empty glass mason jars or containers and close the lid tightly.

Beeswax

Bees use wax to construct the cells of the combs, which you can harvest once bees make use of it in around three to five years. The cell cappings are also made of wax that you can further strain when harvesting honey. Most people use beeswax by rendering it for other products. Hives that did not make it or bees that left the hive will have left beeswax that we can clean to create other products as well.

Rendering

Rendering is the process of separating fat from oil and other forms of debris. In this process, we render beeswax by separating honey and solid material from the wax itself.

How to render beeswax:

1. Clean the beeswax with running water and break it up into smaller pieces.
2. Let it dry for a while.
3. Put it in a skillet or any metal container you can heat.
4. Fill half the container with water and a cheesecloth to separate debris.
5. Keep adding more beeswax while it melts and set it aside for a few hours.
6. The hard wax will settle on top floating.
7. Remove the wax and heat it again.
8. Before it hardens, strain the liquid wax into any mold or container.
9. Set it aside for future use.

Beekeeping Benefits

Health

Beekeeping is not only an activity people do to acquire honey for its health benefits, but also for a sense of fulfillment.

The high antioxidant quality of honey helps us battle illnesses, improves the immune system, and lowers blood pressure and cholesterol. As a sweetener, it is also good for your heart. If you cut yourself while working in the field, you can grab some fresh honey and rub it on the wound.

Raw honey improves your metabolism, mood and sleep pattern. You can even use it as a face wash. Many women use it as a natural beauty agent to remove blackheads and pimples.

Beekeeping is an outdoor hobby. It will get you stretching your muscles. Lifting heavy boxes, doing inspections, and regularly attending to your hives makes for some good mild exercise.

Royal jelly, propolis and protein from the pollen are great sources of nutrients. Most of these products are used by pharmaceutical companies. This is why professionals and major industries go into the bee business.

Economic Returns

Even as a first year beekeeper, you can make profits with only one or two hives. You will not make that much honey in your first year. If you have been diligent, you can harvest $15 to $30 per hive in your first year.

However, there are other ways to expand your bee business, such as selling your bee colonies as sources to other beekeepers by splitting colonies, building hives, collecting and selling pollen and a whole lot more.

Conclusion

Your beekeeping practices will improve as the years go by. You will also learn how to apply different management techniques to increase the number of your colonies. Modern beekeepers buy flow-hives instead of the usual practice.

Even though there are more management activities that you need to learn, this book has given you the knowledge you need to start beekeeping. Most of these practices require years of experience to guarantee success.

Overall, beekeeping is a practice that provides an excellent sense of fulfillment. We get to watch the short yet significant lives of insects that are extremely helpful to our existence as human beings.

If you've enjoyed reading this book, subscribe* to my mailing list for exclusive content and sneak peaks of my future books.

Visit the link below:

http://eepurl.com/glvBjj

OR

Use the QR Code:

(*Must be 13 years or older to subscribe)

Printed in Great Britain
by Amazon